CHRIS LANE

GET ON-LINE
CRE@TE YOUR OWN WEB SITE

BLOOMSBURY

Produced by

Patricia Borlenghi Book Packaging,
157 Highbury Hill, London N5 1TB

Designed by tribal

Cover design by Michelle Radford

Copyright

All rights reserved; no part of this publication may be
reproduced or transmitted by any means, electronic,
mechanical, photocopying or otherwise, without the
prior permission of the publisher
First published in Great Britain in 1998
Bloomsbury Publishing Plc,
38 Soho Square, London W1V 5DF
Copyright © Text Chris Lane and Patricia Borlenghi 1998
The moral rights of the authors have been asserted
A CIP catalogue record of this book is available from the
British Library
ISBN 0 7475 3979 0.
Printed in Great Britain
10 9 8 7 6 5 4 3 2 1

Acknowledgements

All trademarks are acknowledged to be the property of their
respective owners.
Thanks to Allie Holly, Keisuke Ueda, Sophie Winsley, Poppy St
James, Derya Davenport, Nigel Lee and Bronwyn Lee.

contents

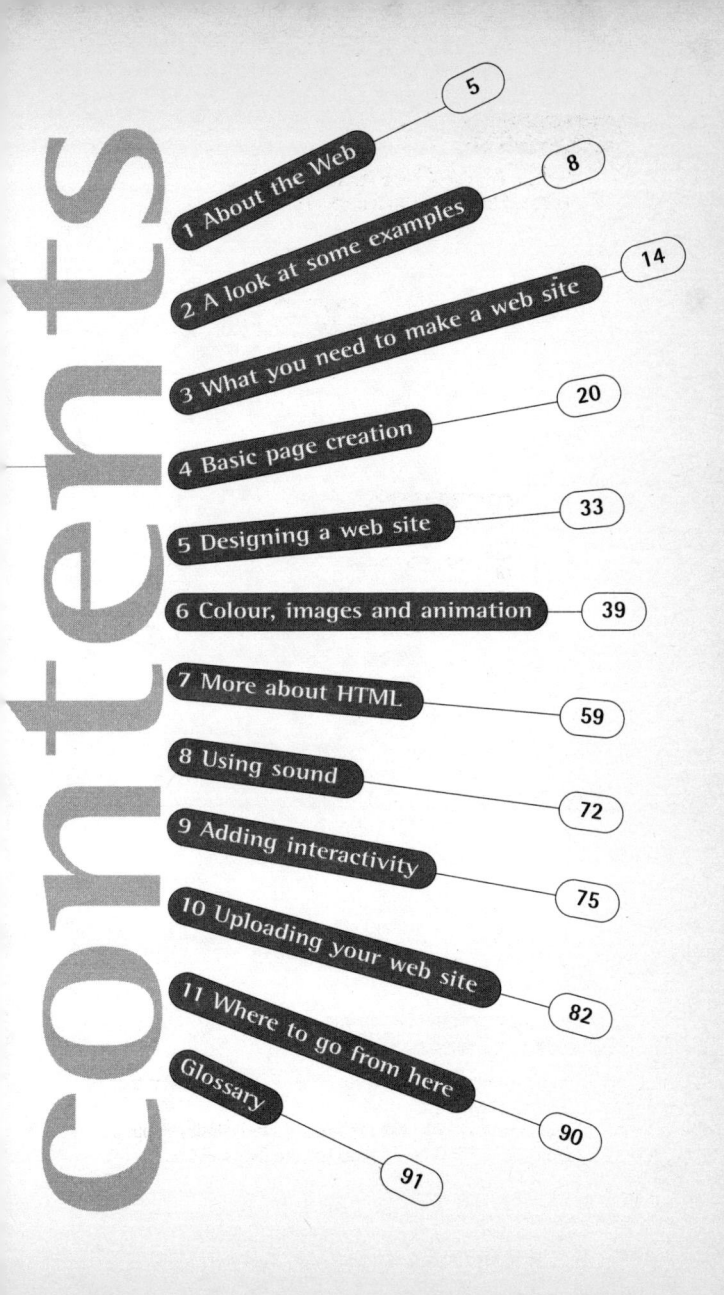

1 About the Web — 5
2 A look at some examples — 8
3 What you need to make a web site — 14
4 Basic page creation — 20
5 Designing a web site — 33
6 Colour, images and animation — 39
7 More about HTML — 59
8 Using sound — 72
9 Adding interactivity — 75
10 Uploading your web site — 82
11 Where to go from here — 90
Glossary — 91

chapter 1

About the web

The *World Wide Web* makes it possible for you to publish your work so that anyone in the world with a personal computer can look at it.

Creating a basic *web page* is not difficult. All you need is a computer, access to the Internet and a bit of imagination. Once you've made your pages, it can cost next to nothing to get them 'on-line'.

The World Wide Web is part of the *Internet* and was invented in 1989 by Tim Berners-Lee. It is a system for creating *Hypertext* documents that can all be linked together.

Today the *Web* is one of the most popular parts of the Internet. It is changing our lives, just as the printing press and the telephone did when they were invented.

You can use the web for a range of exciting activities. This book will show you some of them.

Who this book is for

Anyone wanting to learn how to make web pages at home or at school will find this book helpful. It is also for families who want to learn how to use computers together. Some knowledge of word processing and browsing the Internet before you begin would be helpful.

Software used in this book

The examples given in this book are for Windows 95/98. But you can apply what you are learning with similar software on an Apple Macintosh or a PC with Windows 3.1 as well.

Safety and security on the Internet

If you are creating pages on the Internet, you need to think about being safe. There are some simple rules that you should always follow:

- Don't agree to meet anybody whom you have contacted over the Internet without taking a responsible adult with you.
- Always tell adults who are responsible for you about how you are using the Internet and about anything that you feel unhappy or unsure about.

about the web

- Don't give out your home address, phone number, or any credit card details over the Internet without discussing it first with a responsible adult.

Important words throughout this book are in *italics*. Look up the Glossary at the end to find out more.

Next we will see some examples of what people are actually doing on the Web.

chapter 2

A look at some examples

Before you think about making your own web site, it will be helpful to see how other web site designers are getting their ideas across. You can find all of these pages by entering the addresses shown for each person into a web browser.

Allie Holly's pages have links to her favourite web sites.

- 138.25.70.111/home/allie/index.htm#Top

Welcome to my Homepage!

Allie's Home Page

- Please Sign My New Guest Book
- Things I Like
- Things I Dislike
- My Favourite Books - check out my new and improved BOOKS page! LOTS of my favourite books with short reviews and many links to related sites.
- My Favourite T.V. Shows
- My Favourite Movies
- Some Of My Favourite Toys
- On-Line Clubs I Belong To
- Awards I Have Won
- Links To My Favourite Web Sites
- About Australia - lots of great information links about Sydney, Australia too.
- L👀K Here to see Allie in my dancing concert costume - I played the Black Sheep in "Babe".
- L👀K Here To See A Photo Of Me and My Barbie® Collection.
- L👀K Here to see my Tuttie doll in her Play Case. Tuttie is one of my favourite dolls.
- L👀K Here These are 3 of my favourite Vintage Dolls

Family-Friendly Site™

this site meets all reqt's at www.virtuocity.com/family.html

a look at some examples

9

Keisuke's pages include some interesting icons.

- www.tama.or.jp/~adeu/keisuke/index.html

Sophie Winsley's pages begin with an introduction to the Isle of Man where she lives. Sophie also includes a message for you to 'come back soon'.

- homepages.enterprise.net/ted.hall/sophie.html

Poppy's Warrior Princess pages include her own drawings and stories.

- www.flatearth.co.uk/poppy

Derya has made some beautiful section headings.

- www.cs.bilkent.edu.tr/~derya/derya.html

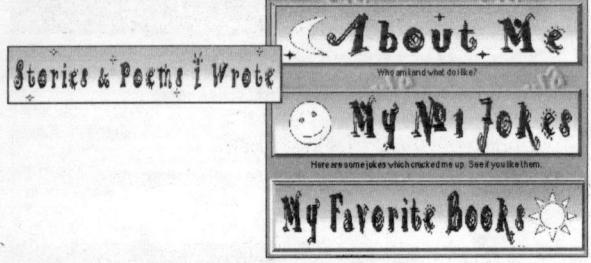

Nigel has included lots of football information on his pages.

- nigel.group.com.hk/nigeland

a look at some examples

This is an example of an imaginative *background* image from Bronwyn Lee.
- www-personal.usyd.edu.au/~mslee/bronwyn.html

Now have a look at Angelo's pages.

They will be used as examples throughout this book. To look them up go to: •www.bloomsbury.com/websitebook

With Angelo's pages we will find out about:

Creating text, images and animations.

Making links and including *multimedia* files.

Creating different sections for your *web site*.

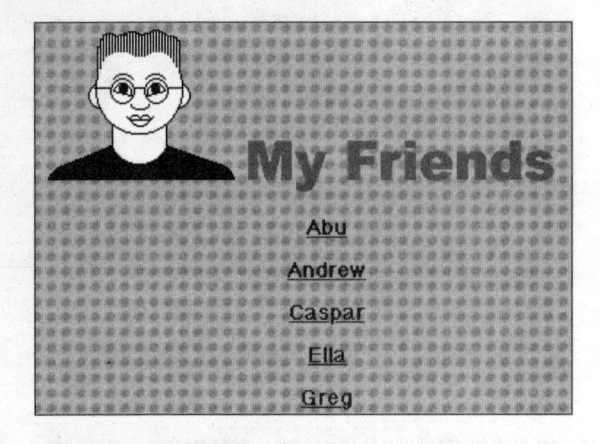

a look at some examples

Setting the way that text and graphics are arranged on the page.

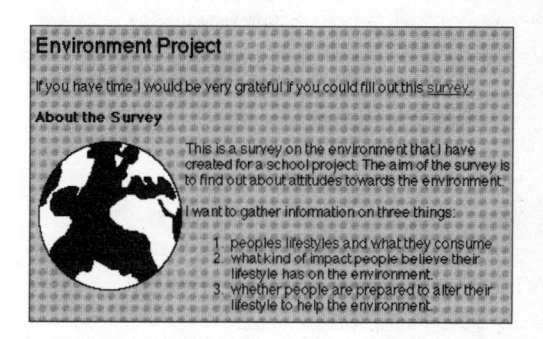

Making *forms* for *visitors* to fill in.

Now that we have seen some examples of other web sites, it's time to get hold of what you need to create your own pages.

chapter 3
What you need to make a web site

In this chapter you will find out about what you need before you can start to create a web page. The basics include a computer with a *modem*, a web *browser*, an *HTML* editor and an image editing programme.

Computer hardware

Any computer that is able to run Netscape Navigator or Microsoft Internet Explorer can make web pages. You will also need a modem, a sound card and microphone, and an account with an *Internet Service Provider* (ISP). See chapter 10 for details.

Computer operating systems

You might be thinking about buying a computer for making web pages. If you are, the main choice is between the Apple Macintosh and a PC with Windows 95/98. Both kinds of machine are suitable. You can also make pages with Windows 3.1.

HTML Specifications

The Language used to create web pages is called *Hyper Text Markup Language* or HTML. It is made up of codes that say which parts of a page will have headings or pictures and which parts will be plain text. When your page arrives on someone else's computer, it will need to be understood by their browser.

what you need to make a web site

So there are rules that have been agreed for writing HTML. These rules are written down in the HTML Specifications. Although the specifications are a bit technical, they can be useful because they explain all the code options in great detail.

The most recent specification for HTML is version 4. The HTML specifications can be downloaded from www.w3.org/TR/REC-html40

W3C

HTML 4.0 Specification
W3C Recommendation 18-Dec-1997

Software

In this section, you will find details of where to download the software needed for the examples in this book. If you have difficulty getting hold of any of it, try visiting our web site at: www.bloomsbury.com/websitebook for the latest information.

Browsers

Browsers are the software that let you view web pages. The most popular web browsers are Netscape Navigator, and Microsoft Internet Explorer.

MicroSoft Internet Explorer

- Macintosh and Windows • Free
- www.microsoft.com/ie

Internet Explorer

Netscape Communicator
- Macintosh and Windows • Free
- home.netscape.com/download

HTML

There are two ways to create HTML. The easy way is with software that lets you see how web pages will actually appear, as you are working. These kind of programmes are sometimes called *WYSIWYG* editors. This stands for 'What You See Is What You Get'. You don't have to learn HTML code to make web pages this way.

The difficult way is with software that only displays your pages in code form. Examples of HTML editing software include:

MicroSoft FrontPage
- WYSIWYG • Macintosh and Windows
- -www.microsoft.com/frontpage

MicroSoft FrontPage Express
- WYSIWYG • Windows only • Free
- -www.micosoft.com/ie
- Comes packaged with Internet Explorer

Netscape Composer
- WYSIWYG • Free • Macintosh and Windows
- home.netscape.com/download
- Comes packaged with Netscape Navigator 4

Adobe PageMill
- WYSIWYG • Macintosh and Windows
- www.adobe.com/prodindex/pagemill

what you need to make a web site

Claris Homepage
- WYSIWYG • Macintosh and Windows
- www.claris.com/software

MacroMedia DreamWeaver
- Version 4 HTML • Macintosh and Windows
- WYSIWYG
- www.macromedia.com/software/dreamweaver

BBEdit
- Macintosh only • used by professionals
- includes a glossary of all HTML code
- web.barebones.com/products/bbedit/bbedit.html

NoteTab
- Windows only • includes a glossary of HTML code
- www.notetab.ch

Ordinary text editors
Any text editor can be used to create HTML. NotePad for Windows or SimpleText for the Macintosh are examples.

Extensions to existing programmes
Many programmes come with extensions that allow them to create HTML. This is a link to a free HTML converter for MicroSoft Word called Internet Assistant.
- www.microsoft.com/word

Image Editors
No self-respecting web page is complete without images. Popular software includes:

PaintShop Pro
Windows only • www.jasc.com

Adobe PhotoShop

- used by professionals • Macintosh and Windows
- www.adobe.com/prodindex/photoshop

Adobe PhotoDeluxe

- free with scanners and cameras.
- Macintosh and Windows
- www.adobe.com/prodindex/photodeluxe

Animations can help to jazz up your website. The best GIF animation programmes are:

GIF builder • Macintosh only
- tucows.cableinet.net/mac/imganimac.html

Ulead GIF Animator • Windows only
- www.ulead.com

Image mappers are programmes that let you set how regions of an image will link to other pages

MapEdit • Windows and Macintosh
- www.boutell.com/mapedit

Multimedia software

There are many additional file formats that can be used on web pages. Some of the most popular programmes are: Macromedia Flash, Director and Adobe Premiere.

Sound can add another dimension to your pages:

GoldWave • Windows • www.goldwave.com

SoundEffects • Macintosh
- www.riccisoft.com/soundeffects/

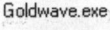

what you need to make a web site

FTP software

When you have completed your pages you will need FTP software to move them onto the Internet.

CuteFTP • Windows •www.globalscape.net

Fetch • Macintosh
•tucows.cableinet.net/mac/ftpmac.html

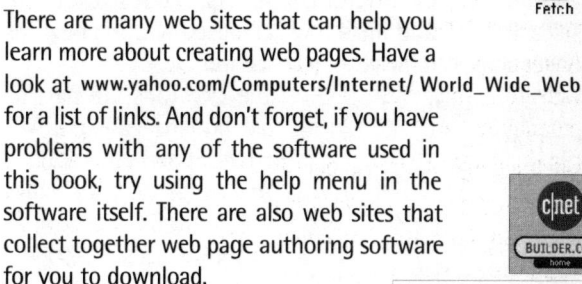

There are many web sites that can help you learn more about creating web pages. Have a look at www.yahoo.com/Computers/Internet/ World_Wide_Web for a list of links. And don't forget, if you have problems with any of the software used in this book, try using the help menu in the software itself. There are also web sites that collect together web page authoring software for you to download.
Tucows www.tucows.com and CNet www.cnet.com are examples.

The software used in this book can be downloaded over the Internet. Most of it is either free or can be used for a trial period before paying for it. The recommended software is listed below.

Windows 95/98: NotePad, MicroSoft Internet Explorer 4 (including FrontPage Express) PaintShop Pro 5, Ulead GIF animator 2, GoldWave 4 and CuteFTP 2.

Macintosh: SimpleText, Netscape Communicator (including Composer), PhotoShop 5 or PhotoDeluxe 2, GifBuilder 0.5, SoundEffects 0.9.2 and Fetch 3.

Now you're ready to start making your first page.

chapter 4
Basic page creation

This chapter will explain how to create some very simple web pages. The pages you make will contain text of different sizes, images and links to other pages.

Understanding basic HTML

The first thing to understand about web pages is that there are two ways of viewing them.

One is the way that visitors see them when they are browsing – as page layouts with images and text. The other is the way they appear when you create them, with special codes that are enclosed within chevrons < and >.

The chevrons are part of a language called HTML. HTML allows you to make the words on your pages bold or italic or appear at different sizes. It also lets you include images in pages and create Hypertext links. A piece of HTML code is called a *Tag*.

```
<HTML>

<HEAD>
<TITLE>Angelo's Page</TITLE>
</HEAD>

<BODY>
Welcome to Angelo's Home Page
</BODY>

</HTML>
```

This illustration shows the code in a very basic page made in SimpleText on the Macintosh.

Welcome to Angelo's Home page

This illustration shows the resulting web page after it has been opened into Netscape Navigator.

Many tags have *Attributes* that control what they do.

It is important to notice that most tags come in pairs. <HEAD> and </HEAD> are examples. Each pair of tags have an effect on the information that appears between them. The second tag in the pair always uses the '/' character.

We said that there are two ways of creating HTML.

We will begin with the 'difficult' way – but don't worry - it's pretty easy really. Later, you will learn how to work faster by using a WYSIWYG editor.

What you will need before you begin

You should install MicroSoft Internet Explorer 4 or Netscape Communicator 4 on to your computer's hard disk. You should also understand how to switch between different programmes. In Windows 95/98 you can use the task bar. On the Macintosh use the Application menu.

All the examples in this chapter are for Internet Explorer. The main difference between Navigator and Explorer is the name given to the button which allows you to view changes to your pages.

In Explorer the button is called 'refresh'.
In Navigator the button is called 'reload'.

Typing in text and code

To begin creating your page you will need to open a text editing program. If you are using Windows you should use *NotePad*. If you are working on a Macintosh use SimpleText.

From the Start menu, choose Programmes, Accessories and *NotePad*.

When you open *NotePad* a new blank document appears on the screen. Type in the text that you can see below: start with <HTML> and end with </HTML>. Take special care to enter any text that appears between two chevrons < > exactly as it is shown here. The smallest mistake can make the entire document fail to display correctly.

```
<HTML>

<HEAD>
<TITLE>Angelo's Page</TITLE>
</HEAD>

<BODY>
Welcome to Angelo's Home Page
</BODY>

</HTML>
```

Any words that fall outside the chevrons can be changed. So where you see 'Angelo's Page' and 'Welcome to Angelo's Home Page' you can write your own name, or anything else you like.

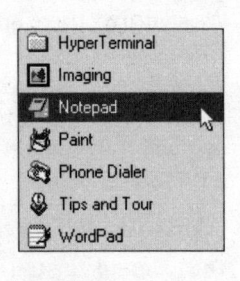

What the tags mean.

The <HTML> tag is used to begin and end a web page.

The <HEAD> tag is used to hold information that is not part of the page content.

The <TITLE> tag contains the text that will appear in the title bar of the web page window.

The <BODY> tag contains all the content of the page including text and images.

Saving work and previewing your page

Choose 'Save' from the 'File' menu. Save your document on the desktop for now.

The naming of the file is very important. You must make sure that it has '.htm' written onto the end. This is called a *suffix* and helps the browser to understand what kind of document is being loaded.

It is also important to select 'Text Documents' as the file type. Next click the 'Save' button.

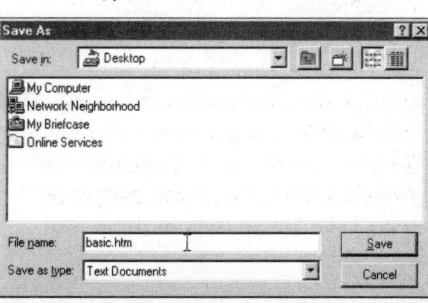

Next open Internet Explorer from the 'Start' menu. Then choose 'Open' from the 'File' menu.

Click the 'Browse' button and choose the file that we have just created in *NotePad*. In the open dialogue box the file is called 'basic'. Don't worry if the '.htm' is missing from the file name – Windows 95/98 is often set to make the suffixes invisible. Click 'Open'.

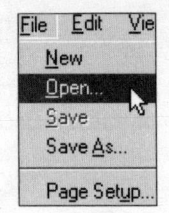

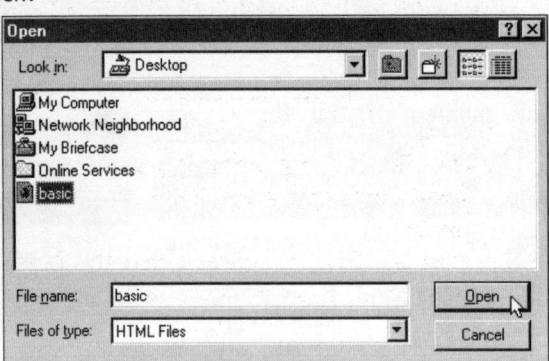

In the next box click 'OK'.

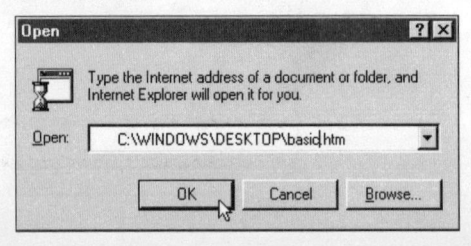

basic page creation

The page you have created is displayed in the browser.

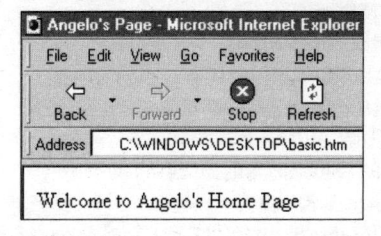

```
Angelo's Page - Microsoft Internet Explorer
File  Edit  View  Go  Favorites  Help
Back   Forward   Stop   Refresh
Address  C:\WINDOWS\DESKTOP\basic.htm

Welcome to Angelo's Home Page
```

Creating links

Now you are going to make some additions to the page. Click '*NotePad*' on the task bar. The text editor appears.

`basic - Notepad`

Add the tag <A HREF= "basic2.htm"> About my family </A>. The purpose of this tag is to make the words 'About my family' act as a link to a new file called 'basic2.htm'.
In this piece of HTML 'A' indicates that this is the *Anchor* tag. 'HREF' is an attribute of 'A' and sets which page the link will lead to.

```
<HTML>

<HEAD>
<TITLE>Angelo's Page</TITLE>
</HEAD>

<BODY>

Welcome to Angelo's Home Page

<A HREF="basic2.htm">About my family</A>

</BODY>

</HTML>
```

Notice that some text on the web page is in capitals and some is not. HTML tags are often written in *upper case*, but they don't have to be. File names are more of a problem. The Internet sees *lower case* and *upper case* file names as different.
'Angelo.htm' is not the same file as 'angelo.htm'. The use of upper case and lower case in a link from a web page must match the file name itself. For this reason it is best to use lower case only in file names, to avoid confusion.

Save the document.

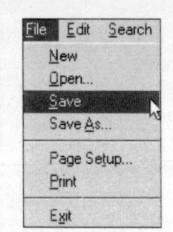

File	Edit	Search
New		
Open...		
Save		
Save As...		
Page Setup...		
Print		
Exit		

Switch to 'Internet Explorer'.

Angelo's Page - Microsoft

The page in 'Explorer' is not yet showing the changes that you have made.

Press the 'Refresh' button

Refresh

The change that you have made is now displayed.

Now try to click on the blue underlined text. This is a link to the document 'basic2.htm'.

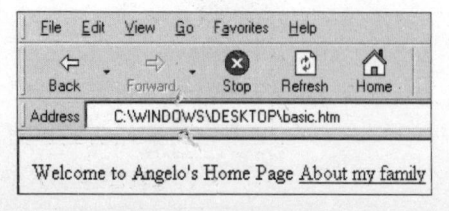

File	Edit	View	Go	Favorites	Help

⇐ Back	⇒ Forward	✕ Stop	↻ Refresh	⌂ Home

Address C:\WINDOWS\DESKTOP\basic.htm

Welcome to Angelo's Home Page <u>About my family</u>

basic page creation

You will see the following message. 'The system cannot find the file specified'. This is because the new page has not yet been created.

Microsoft Internet Explorer
Internet Explorer cannot open the Internet site C:\WINDOWS\DESKTOP\basic2.htm.
The system cannot find the file specified.

Click 'OK'

To create the page switch back to your text editor.

Now we are going to create a second page based on the first.

Select 'Save As' from the 'File' menu.

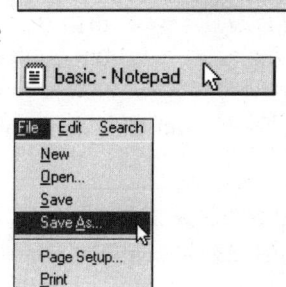

Name the file 'basic2.htm'.

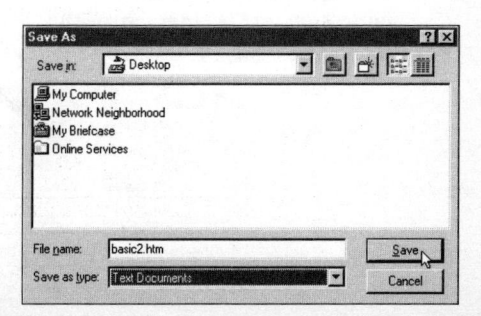

Make the changes shown. Notice that the link is now pointing back at the original page 'basic.htm'.

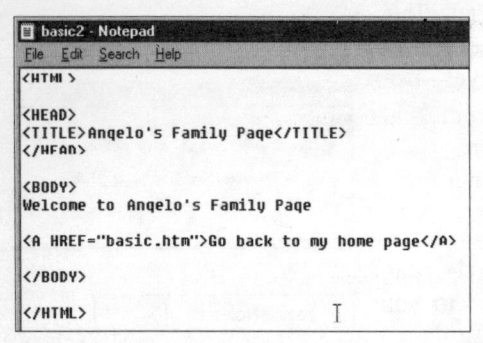

```
basic2 - Notepad
File  Edit  Search  Help
<HTML >

<HEAD>
<TITLE>Angelo's Family Page</TITLE>
</HEAD>

<BODY>
Welcome to Angelo's Family Page

<A HREF="basic.htm">Go back to my home page</A>

</BODY>

</HTML>
```

Select 'Save' from the 'File' menu. Switch to 'Explorer'.

Angelo's Page - Microsol...

File menu:
- New
- Open...
- Save
- Save As...
- Page Setup...
- Print
- Exit

The first page is still displayed in 'Explorer'.
But now when you click on the link 'About my family', instead of displaying an error message, the browser displays 'basic2.htm'.

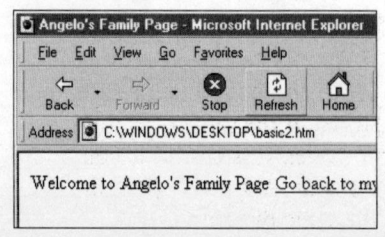

```
Angelo's Family Page - Microsoft Internet Explorer
File  Edit  View  Go  Favorites  Help

 ⇐       ⇒       ⊗      ↻        ⌂
Back  Forward   Stop  Refresh   Home

Address  C:\WINDOWS\DESKTOP\basic2.htm

Welcome to Angelo's Family Page  Go back to my
```

Using relative and absolute links

There are two ways to create links to other pages. The method used in the example is a *relative link*. The second kind of link is an *absolute link*.

Absolute links

Absolute links usually link to pages somewhere else on the Internet. Absolute links look like this:

`<AHREF="http://another.web.server/my_friends_page/index.htm">`

Notice that the entire address, or *Uniform Resource Locator* (URL), for the document is given including the *protocol* 'http://'.

Relative links

A relative link is used to make links between your own pages. Relative references look like this:

`<A HREF="my_page_2.htm">`

This example is a link between pages that are stored in the same directory or folder. It is easiest if you save all your web files in the same directory.

The advantage of relative references is that you can change the location of all your pages from your home computer to your web server, and the links between them will still work.

Adding line breaks

Now switch back to the text editor and add the <P> and <BR> tags.

```
<HTML>

<HEAD>
<TITLE>Angelo's Family Page</TITLE>
</HEAD>

<BODY>
Welcome to Angelo's Family Page

<P>

<A HREF="basic.htm">Go back to my <BR>home page</A>

</BODY>
```

'Save' the document.

Switch back to 'Explorer'

'Refresh' the page.

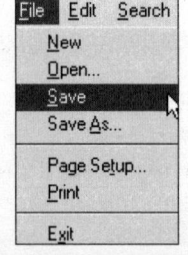

basic page creation

You can see that <P> creates a new paragraph and <BR> causes a line break.

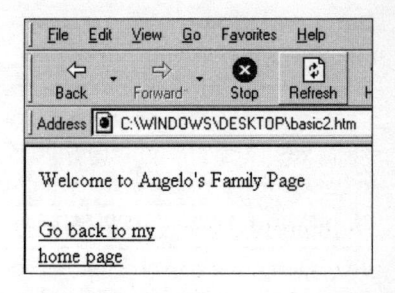

```
File  Edit  View  Go  Favorites  Help
 ⇦       ⇨        ⊗        ↻
Back   Forward   Stop    Refresh
Address  C:\WINDOWS\DESKTOP\basic2.htm

Welcome to Angelo's Family Page

Go back to my
home page
```

Aligning text and inserting images

Reopen 'basic.htm' in NotePad. In the 'Open' dialogue box, view files of type 'All files (*.*)'. Now add the <CENTER> tag (note American spelling) and the <IMG> tag. 'SRC' is an attribute of 'IMG' and it sets the file name of the image that will be used. Also add the <Font> and two <P> tags.

```
<HTML>

<HEAD>
<TITLE>Angelo's Page</TITLE>
</HEAD>

<BODY>

<CENTER>

Welcome to <FONT SIZE="+10">Angelo's</FONT> Home Page <P>

<IMG SRC="angelo.gif" >

<A HREF="basic2.htm">

<P>About my family</A>

</CENTER>

</BODY>

</HTML>
```

Reopen 'basic.htm' in Explorer.

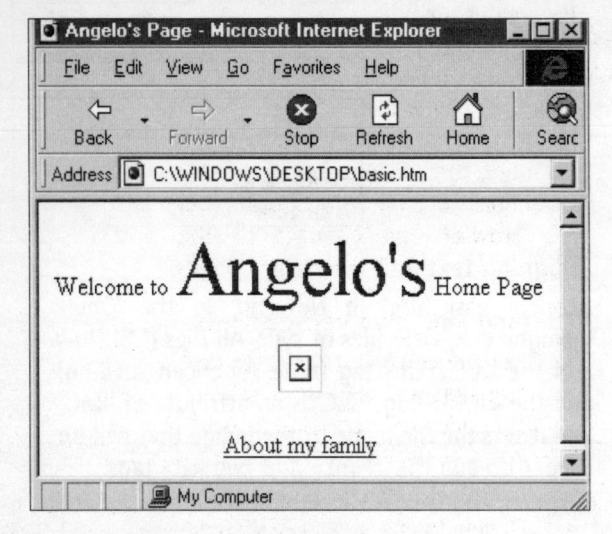

The result is a page where all the elements are centred and an empty square appears that should contain an image. The image is not displaying because we haven't created one yet.

Well done, now you have created your first web pages. Next you are going to plan your own web site.

chapter 5

Designing a web site

We will now think about the web site that you are going to create during the rest of the book. To follow some of the instructions you will need to open your web browser and connect to the Internet.

Creating your own house style

When you are creating a web page it is important that you plan what will go into your pages and decide on a visual style.

A *house style* is a set of design rules that will help to give your web site an identity. It can also speed up the creation of each page because buttons and borders can be used again and again on different pages. Have a look back at Derya's headings in chapter 2. Derya has created many headings that are all in the same style.

Your house style might tell you how you will use typefaces, colours, page layout, pictures, photographs, backgrounds, textures, borders, buttons, headings and rules.

How web pages differ from paper

Before we go on, you need to realise that web pages are very different to working on paper or with desktop publishing software.

When a web page displays, its appearance will vary depending on the size of the browser window.

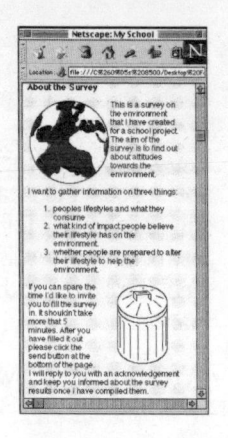

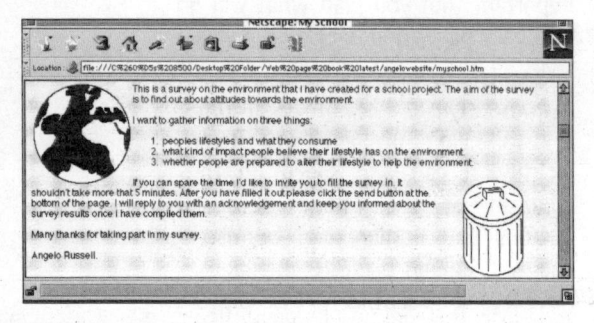

The illustrations show two windows, one wide and one tall. The same information fits onto both pages but in a different way. This happens automatically when the size of the browser window is changed.

The main thing that affects the size of the browser window is the size of the computer screen. If you want to be sure that an image will appear on most screens, it should be no bigger than about 600 *pixels* by 400 pixels. It is possible to create images that are bigger than this, but the viewer may have to scroll their browser window to see them in full.

Another problem is that type faces and type sizes can look different on other people's computers.

When you are designing your pages you'll need to work out how to get around these problems. Try resizing your browser window now to see how this affects the layout of a page.

You'll want to make sure that your designs make good use of colour. When you choose a background colour be careful that it contrasts with the foreground text, otherwise the words will be difficult to read.

You also need to think about what your web site will contain.

Here are some ideas:
- a local magazine
- a homepage for yourself
- a project on the environment in your area
- information about your school
- a gallery of your pictures
- stories that you have written
- links to your friends' web pages
- a map of your neighbourhood
- feature articles
- profiles
- a questionnaire

You should spend some time thinking about *interactive* design. To begin with you will need a *home page*. This is the page that visitors will see first. Home pages provide a starting point for exploring a web site. They should also make an impact and give an idea of what the rest of your pages will contain. And they mustn't take up too much space, definitely no more that 30k (kilobytes).

a navigational pathway that gives the viewer a recommended route through your pages. Forwards and backwards links would be needed to move from one page to the next.

Decide whether you will provide backwards and forwards buttons to take visitors on a recommended route. How will you let them know where they are in your web site?

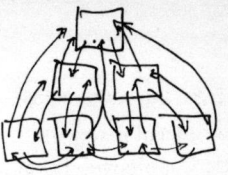

designing a web site

You can help them if they get lost, by creating a link back to your first page from every page on your web site. Decide where you will position buttons so that they are easy to see.

you should try to work out where all the links between each page will lead.

How will you divide your web site up so that a viewer doesn't to have scroll too far through one page?

a very long page. This would need targets or bookmarks to help the viewer move around the page (see chapter 6).

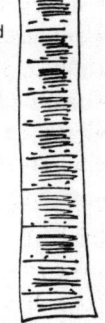

Structuring your web site

There are two main choices that you can make about the structure of your web site.

The very simplest structure is where one page leads to the next and the only direction to move is forwards to the next or backwards to the previous one. This is called a *linear* structure and is suitable for stories or instructions.

There is another structure that is often used in web sites where the viewer is given more choice. This is often called a *hierarchic* structure.

Now you need to draw out a structure for your web site starting with the home page.

a simple hierachic structure.

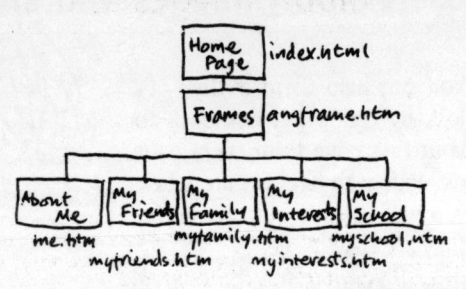

Make some rough sketches of how text and graphics will fit together on each page. Have a look at the illustrations on this page to get some ideas. Finally, think about the names that you will use for your images and files. Try to be systematic and well organised with the names that you choose. Have a look at chapter 10 to get an idea of some other things to consider when naming files.

If you've finished your plan you've completed the first step in the creation of your web site. Next we're going to find out about how to create images and animations.

Angelo's web site showing links and file names.

a sketch for a page layout that includes a left and right frame.

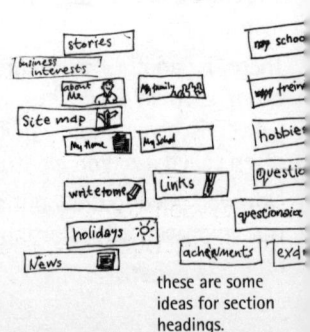

these are some ideas for section headings.

chapter 6
Colour, images and animation

This chapter looks at using images on your web pages and working with colour.

Image file sizes

Images make web pages more exciting. But they also cause problems. They take much longer to travel over the Internet than text files. If it takes too long for someone to see your images, they may give up and go to look at someone else's pages instead.

Many techniques have been developed to squeeze images into a smaller space. One important technique is to keep the width and height of an image down. Another method is called *Compression* and stores data in less space. There are two main image formats for the Web: *JPEG* and *GIF*. Both formats use compression. The table (see next page) gives a comparison between them:

GIF

- allows up to 256 colours
- suitable for flat colour graphics
- allows part of an image to be transparent
- allows you to have full control over how an image's colours are displayed
- once downloaded to your computer, displays quickly on the screen
- GIF images end in '.gif'
- GIF stands for 'Graphics Interchange Format'

JPEG

- allows up to 16 million colours
- suitable for photographs
- can't be transparent
- may look grainy on a screen set to 256 colours
- once downloaded to your computer, displays more slowly on the screen
- JPEG images end in '.jpg' or '.jpeg'
- JPEG stands for 'Joint Photographers Expert Group'

Colour on the Web

Colour on the Web can be created in two ways. One way is to set the colour of text and backgrounds in HTML. The other is to use images.

To set colour in HTML a numbering system called *hexadecimal* is used. Hexadecimal numbers are not the same as decimal numbers.

colour, images and animation

The best way to understand hexadecimal is to compare it to decimal (see diagram):

You should be able to see that hexadecimal is different to counting up to ten. It uses six new numbers after 9: A, B, C, D, E and F.

Now we will think about how these hexadecimal numbers are used to make colours. Every colour on a web page is made up of three parts or lights: red, green and blue. There is a separate hexadecimal number that sets the level of brightness for each part. In hexadecimal 00 means that a light is fully off, FF means that a light is fully on. To give any colour, three hexadecimal numbers are joined together.

decimal	Hex
0	00
1	01
2	02
3	03
4	04
5	05
6	06
7	07
8	08
9	09
10	0A
11	0B
12	0C
13	0D
14	0E
15	0F
16	10
17	11
18	12
19	13
20	14
21	15
22	16
23	17
24	18
25	19
26	1A
27	1B
28	1C
29	1D
30	1E
31	1F
32	20
33	21
34	22
35	23
36	24
continuing	
-	-
51	33
-	-
102	66
-	-
153	99
-	-
204	CC
-	-
255	FF

Here are some examples:

Red

FF 00 00

This means that the value of red is FF, the value of green is 00 and the value of blue is also 00. The combined effect is red.

Magenta

FF 00 FF

This means that the value of red is FF, the value of green is 00 and the value of blue is FF. The combined effect is magenta - a pink colour.

Here is an example of a hexadecimal code being used on a web page.

<BODY BGCOLOR=#CC0033>. You could add this code to the page you made in chapter 4. It needs to replace the <BODY> tag.

The hash (#) symbol is part of the HTML code and means 'number'. The colour shown in this example is a light orange. Why not try to experiment with different numbers to see the effect they have on a sample page?

Web safe colour

We have already said that Web pages don't necessarily look the same on every computer. One thing that affects the way that images appear is the number of colours that the computer screen is set to display.

If a screen is set to thousands of colours or more, images will usually look the way you intended. If a screen is set to 16 colours or less, images and text colours will often look distorted and there is not much that can be done about it. But if a computer is set to 256 colours, and many are, careful use of hexadecimal can ensure that a colour will always display exactly as you wanted.

There is a set of hexadecimal codes that work well on 256 colour displays. They are all the colours that use the numbers 00, 33, 66, 99, CC and FF. There are 216 of them. Later in this chapter we will see how to use them when we create images. These colours are called 'web safe colours'. You should always try to use them in GIF images and for HTML text and backgrounds.

Getting hold of images

Here are some ideas about where to get hold of images:

- scan them in
- draw using the mouse
- save images from the Internet
- use a clip art library

Choosing an image editing programme

The examples in this chapter use PaintShop Pro 5. If you are using a Macintosh, you can achieve similar results with PhotoShop or PhotoDeluxe.

Setting up the programme to display colour in hexadecimal

Open PaintShop Pro. Set how the programme will display colour information.

Choose 'Preferences' and 'General Programme Preferences' from the 'File' menu.

| Preferences ▶ | General Program Preferences... |

Click the 'Dialogs and Palettes' tab.

Color palette
- ◉ Display colors in RGB format   ○ Decimal display
- ○ Display colors in HSL format   ◉ Hexadecimal display

Choose 'Display colors in RGB format' and 'Hexadecimal display'.

colour, images and animation

Using the web palette to select colours

Download the web palette document from: www.bloomsbury.com/websitebook/palette.gif

Open the file in your web browser and save it to your hard disk. Then open it into PaintShop Pro.

Choose the 'Dropper' tool from the toolbar and move it across the palette image. Notice that the web safe hexadecimal codes appear on the right of the screen. Now you are going to use these colours to create a new image. Choose the colour you want by clicking in the palette image with the 'Dropper' tool.

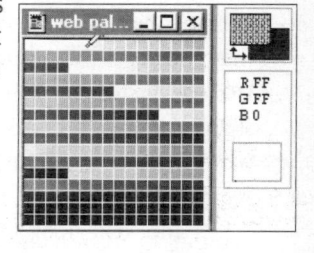

Starting a new file

Choose 'New' from the 'File' menu. We are going to create an image that will contain text that is larger and smoother looking than can be made with HTML.

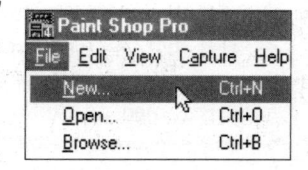

Set the image to 450 pixels wide and 150 pixels high. This is a suitable size for a web page image and is

sometimes called a *banner* heading. Also choose 16.7 million colours and make the background transparent. The DPI should be set to 72.

Click 'OK'

Creating the picture

Click the 'Flood Fill' or 'Paint Bucket' tool. Click in your new image to fill with the colour you chose earlier.

Then use the 'Dropper' to select a new colour from the web palette file.

Select the 'Text' tool. Click on to the new image. Choose a type face and size that you want to use from the next box. Into the panel at the bottom, write the text that you want to use. Make sure that '*anti alias*' is turned on. Anti-aliasing is a process that blends the edge of text so that it doesn't look jagged on the computer screen.

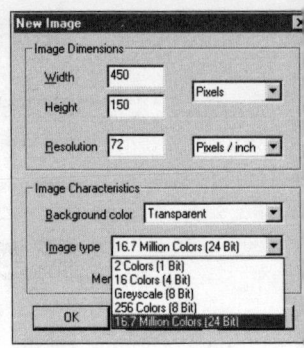

colour, images and animation

Click 'OK'

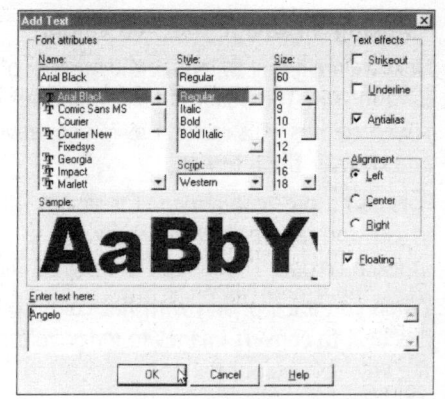

Move the text so that it appears in the middle of the image.

Turn the dotted line selection off by choosing 'Select None' from the 'Selections' menu.

Cropping the image

Use the 'Selection' or 'Marquee' tool and draw a box around the text.

Choose 'Crop to Selection' to make the image smaller.

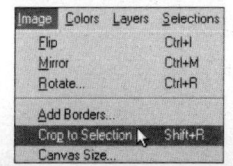

Making an image indexed colour

Next we are going to reduce the number of colours used to store the image. This is important because fewer colours will make the image travel more quickly over the Internet.

It is also a pre-requirement for saving the image in GIF format. The setting we will use is called *indexed colour*.

When you are working with flat colour graphics, it is best to convert images to index colour using the web safe colour palette.

Choose 'Load Palette' from the colour menu.

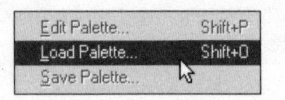

Click 'Yes' to merge layers.

In the next box choose the document 'WEB.pal'.

You can get this file from the Internet at:
www.bloomsbury.co.uk/websitebook/WEB.pal

colour, images and animation

At the bottom of the 'Load Palette' box, choose 'Error diffusion dithering'. This should make the edge of the text stay looking smooth. If the result is too grainy, choose edit and undo and try 'Nearest color matching' instead. Then click 'OK'.

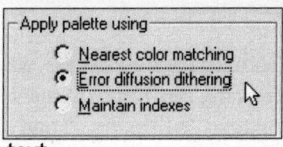

If your image only has a few main colours - like this one - there is a further step to take. The image should have the number of colours in the palette reduced even further. Choose 'Decrease Color Depth' and '16 Colors' from the 'Colors' menu.

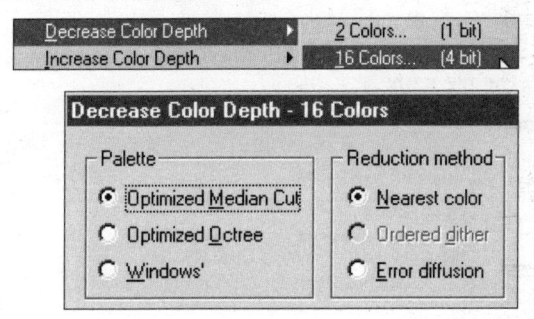

Make the reduction method 'Nearest color'. When you are changing image colours, if you get results that you don't like, select 'Undo' and try again with different settings.

Sometimes you might want to use GIF format for tonal images. In this case, instead of using 'Load Palette', you should convert the colours using 'Decrease Color Depth' and choose '256 colors'.

If you are working in PhotoShop you will need to choose 'Indexed color' from the 'Mode' menu and choose 'Web' from the 'Palette' pop-up menu.

Now choose 'Save As'.

Save	Ctrl+S
Save As...	F12
Save Copy As...	Ctrl+F12

Choose 'CompuServe Graphics Interchange (*.gif)' in the 'Save As type' pop-up menu. Make sure that you include the file suffix '.gif' at the end of the file name.

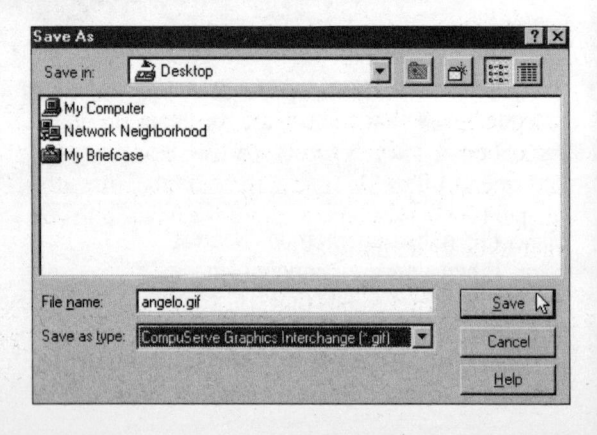

Making a GIF transparent

You can make an image appear to have been cut-out and placed on the background of a web page by making the background transparent. To do this the image must have a background area that is made up of just one colour.

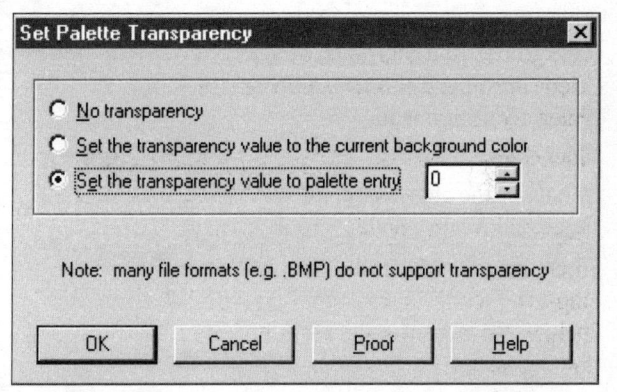

In PaintShop Pro choose 'Set Palette Transparency' from the 'Colors' menu. Then choose 'Set the transparency value to palette entry'. Move the dialogue box so that you can see the image. In Adobe PhotoShop 4, select 'Export' and 'GIF 89A' from the 'File' menu. Then in either programme, use the dropper tool to click on the part of the image that you want to be made transparent.

Then in PaintShop Pro, save the document.

Starting a new JPEG file

JPEG is a file format that is used for photographs and images that have large numbers of shades.

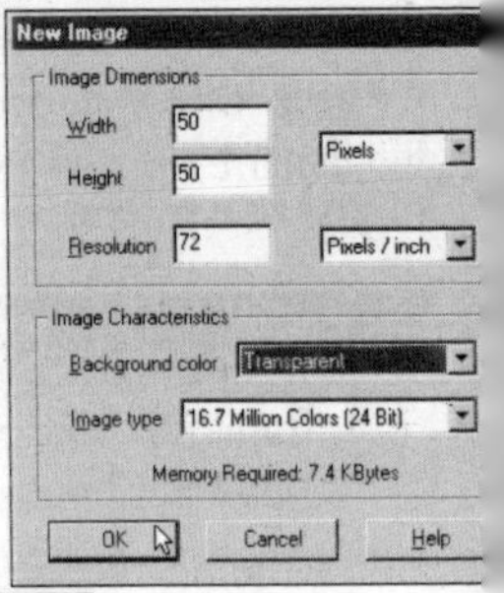

Make an image that is smaller than the first one. In the next chapter we will use it to fill in the background of a web page. Choose 'New' from the 'File' menu. Choose a size for your image.

Click 'OK'.

A new image appears. Fill the image with one colour.

Then draw a dot with the paintbrush tool.

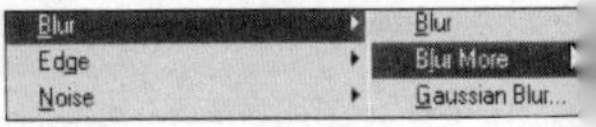

Choose 'Blur' from the 'Image' menu. Do this several times. This helps to create a feeling of depth when the image is displayed in the background.

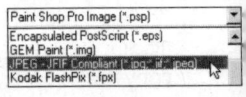

Save the file, choosing JPEG as the file type.

The image can take up less space by clicking 'Options' and choosing a high compression level. The more you compress, the lower the image quality will be. Name the file 'background.jpg'.

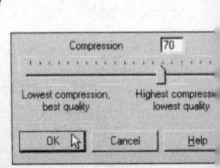

Now you have created two images using the most common image formats on the web – GIF and JPEG.

Creating animated GIFs

Next we are going to create an animated logo. You will need to think up a series of pictures that will work together to show movement. You should sketch them out first.

This example is a picture of Angelo blinking and moving his eyes. There are eight frames and the image is 128 pixels by 102 pixels.

Create the first image by drawing into your image editor. Make the background a contrasting colour. The eyes have been left intentionally blank.

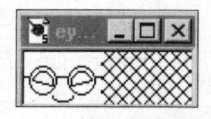

Copy the eye area of the image and choose 'Edit' and 'Paste as new file'. Do this several times and give each file a different name. You should now have a number of identical files.

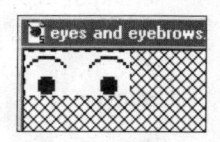

Now we are going to create the eyes and eyebrows as a separate image. When this is done, select them with the 'Lasso' tool and copy the image. Switch to one of the small blank eye images. Choose 'Edit' and 'Paste As Transparent Selection'.

When the cursor moves onto the blank eyes images you will see that the eyes show up on top.

Continue the process so that the eyes are in a slightly different place in each image. Double click to drop the selection when it is where you want it. Leave one of the images with no eyes. Then save all the images

Another idea for creating an animated GIF is to rotate part of the image through 360 degrees.

The animation can then be looped so that it appears to go round indefinitely. Before saving these images, load the web palette as we did earlier in the chapter. Then decrease the number of colours to 16 and choose 'Optimized' and 'Nearest color'.

colour, images and animation

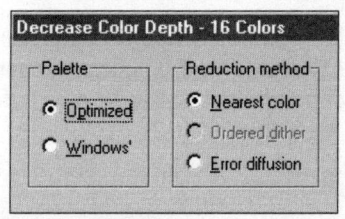

Then make the background transparent as in the earlier example and save as a GIF.

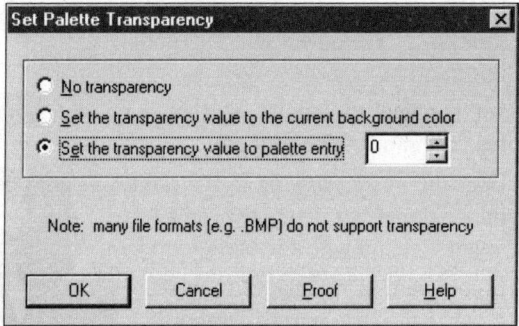

To make the images move we will use Ulead GifAnimator. If you are using a Macintosh, you can use GIFBuilder to achieve similar effects.

Open 'GifAnimator'.

Click 'Blank animation'.

Choose 'Add Images' from the 'Layer' menu.

Select the first image from your animated series – the larger one – and click import. Then repeat the process for the remaining images.

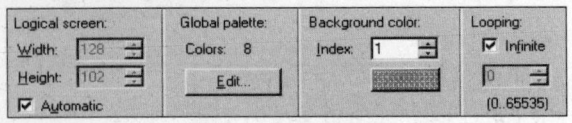

In the panel on the left of the GIF Animator Window, select 'Global Information'.

Set 'Looping' to 'Infinite', so that the animation plays continuously.

Drag the images around in the right hand panel so that the smaller images line up with the background.

If you want some images to appear more than once, select them in the left hand panel, and duplicate them.

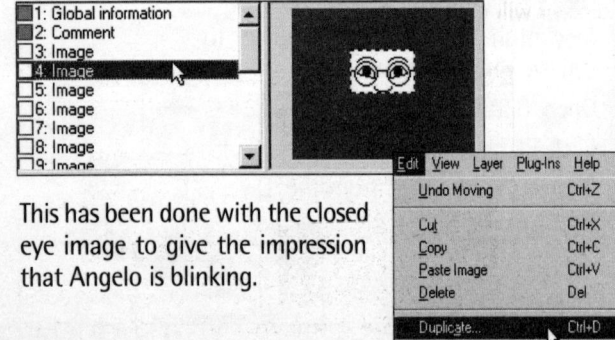

This has been done with the closed eye image to give the impression that Angelo is blinking.

colour, images and animation

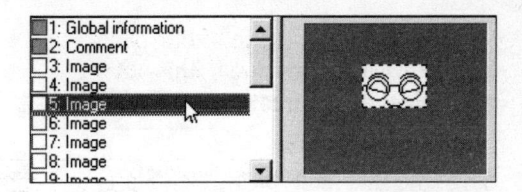

You can also change the order that images appear by dragging them in the left hand panel. In this illustration image 5 is being moved between 7 and 9.

This animation needs a transparent background. Turn 'Interlace off' and 'Transparent index' on.

Select the larger image, then click onto the colour panel next to 'Transparent index'.

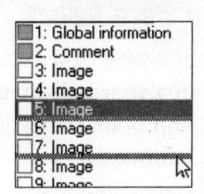

Click on the image to identify which colour will be made transparent.

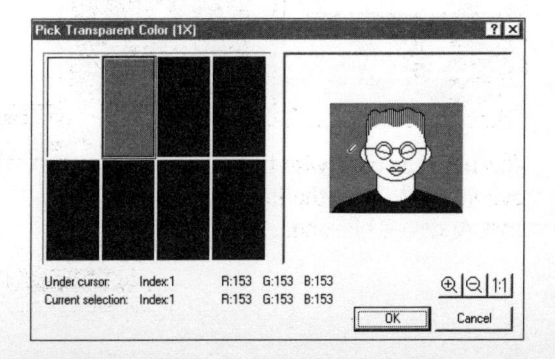

Set 'How to remove' to 'Do not remove' for all the frames. How to remove: Do not remove

Save the file and press the 'Start Preview' button. Start Preview

You may wish to experiment with the 'interframe delay' for the animation to control the speed that it plays.

Once the animation has been created, you can use it just like any other image by using the <IMG> tag in a web page.

Now you've created a GIF, a JPEG image, and an animation. Next we're going to find out some more about HTML.

chapter 7

More about HTML

We have created HTML the difficult way by writing code into a text editor. Now we will look at creating HTML the easy way - with a WYSIWYG editor. For these examples we will use FrontPage Express which comes with Internet Explorer. If you are using a Macintosh, use Netscape Composer. We will also look at some of the HTML that underlies the effects we create. If you want to try entering the HTML directly into a text editor, you can add it anywhere between the <BODY> and </BODY> tags on the pages you made in Chapter 4 using NotePad.

Beginning with FrontPage Express

Open 'FrontPage Express' from the 'Start' menu and select a 'Normal Page'.

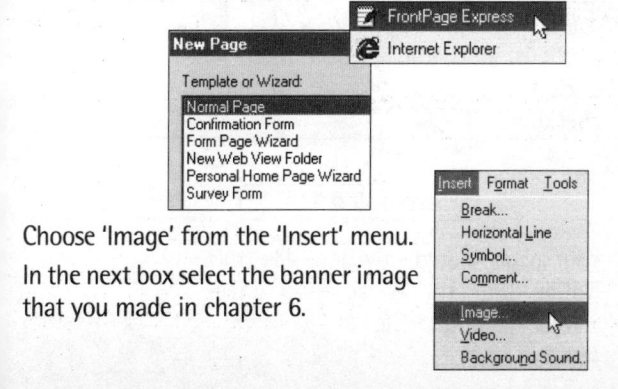

Choose 'Image' from the 'Insert' menu.
In the next box select the banner image that you made in chapter 6.

The image will appear on the page aligned to the left.

Click the 'Centre' button.

Now we will insert the background image we made in chapter 6.

Choose 'Background' from the 'Format' menu. Type in the name of the background file.

At the same time choose a colour that matches the image from the colour pop-up menu. Here a 'web safe' custom colour has been used.

Click the 'Background Image' checkbox.

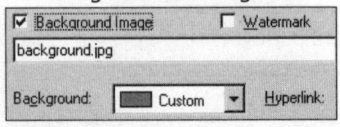

Your page should now look like this. Notice that the background image shows through the text.

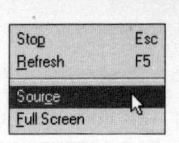

Now select 'Source' from the 'Go' menu. You should see codes that are identical to the ones we wrote by hand in chapter 4.

One of the best ways to learn HTML is to look at other peoples web sites. By viewing the 'Source' you can copy someone else's code into your HTML editor and change it. Try this with Angelo's pages. This can be a good way of learning, but always rearrange the pages to make them your own when you create them this way.

Now save your page and open Internet Explorer. Then open the page into Explorer. Now you can switch between Explorer and FrontPage Express to edit and preview your pages as you work.

Flowing text around an image

Double click an image in FrontPage Express and select the 'Appearance' tab. There are a number of alignment options that control how text flows round images. Flowing text around an image is an attribute of the <IMG> tag. Here is an example <IMG SRC="angelo.gif" ALIGN=RIGHT>.

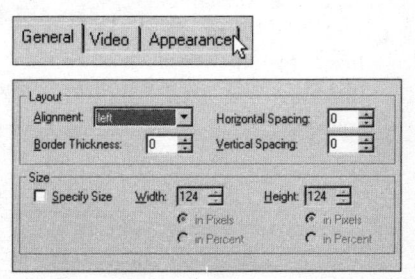

Text and object alignment

You can use the <CENTER> tag to align text and images in the middle of the web page, or the <DIV ALIGN=right> tag, which aligns them to the right. If you don't use either, everything is aligned to the left by default.

In FrontPage Express there is an alignment button on the toolbar.

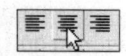

Links in FrontPage Express

You saw how to create a link as HTML code in chapter 4. To make a link in FrontPage Express, select the text or image that you want to make a link from. This is called an Anchor.

Click the 'Link' button on the toolbar.

Type the filename that you want to link to in the dialogue box that follows.

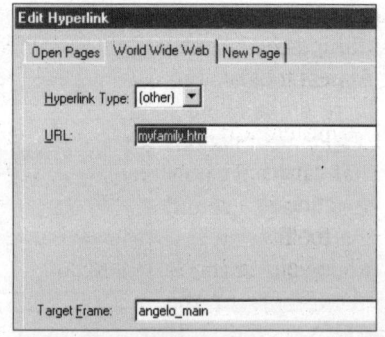

Edit Hyperlink

Open Pages | World Wide Web | New Page |

Hyperlink Type: (other) ▼

URL: myfamily.htm

Target Frame: angelo_main

Click OK and the selected text becomes a link.

My Interests

Bookmarks or Targets

Usually when you follow a link, the top of the new page loads into the browser window. Sometimes, if you have a very long page, it is useful to be able to link to headings further down the page. To do this you can write the following HTML in the place that you want your link to go to: <A Name="survey"></A>. This is called a *Bookmark* or *Target*.

Then, to link to the Bookmark from another page, write:
<A HREF="myschool.htm#survey">go to the survey</A>

Or to go there from another place on the same page, write:
<A HREF="#survey">go to the survey</A>

Indenting text

You can *indent* text from the left margin by clicking the indent button on the FrontPage Express toolbar.

Type colour

You can change the colour of any text by selecting it and clicking the colour tool on the toolbar. Try to use the web safe palette when you are choosing a colour.

Type size

You can increase or decrease the size of individual letters by clicking the 'A' buttons on the toolbar. The HTML equivalents are:

<FONT SIZE=+1>Angelo</FONT>
<FONT SIZE=+2>Angelo</FONT>
<FONT SIZE=+3>Angelo</FONT>
<FONT SIZE=+4>Angelo</FONT>

Style

You can also make text
bold: <STRONG>Angelo</STRONG>
Italic: <EM>Angelo</EM>
or click the style button in FrontPage Express.

Typeface

You can tell a browser which type face you would prefer it to use to show your pages.

<FONT FACE="Arial, Helvetica">

This example makes Arial the first choice and Helvetica the second.

You can select a preferred typeface from the FrontPage Express toolbar.

Heading styles

There is another method for changing the size of type which effects an entire line or paragraph.

\<H1\>Angelo\</H1\> the biggest
\<H2\>Angelo\</H2\>
\<H3\>Angelo\</H3\>
\<H4\>Angelo\</H4\>
\<H5\>Angelo\</H5\>
\<H6\>Angelo\</H6\> the smallest
In FrontPage Express select
'Paragraph from the 'Format' menu.

Rules

Horizontal rules can be written as follows:

\<HR Width="100" Size="2"\>

This rule has a width of 100 pixels and a height of 2.

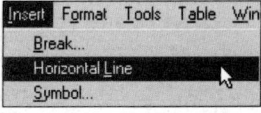

Horizontal rules can be created in FrontPage Express by choosing 'Horizontal Line' from the 'Insert' menu.

Lists

Lists can be created by clicking the List button in FrontPage Express.

The HTML looks like this for a numbered list:

\<OL\>
\<LI\>Apples \</LI\>
\<LI\>Oranges\</LI\>
\<LI\>Pears\</LI\>
\</OL\>

And this for a bulleted list:
```
<OL>
<LI>Apples </LI>
<LI>Oranges</LI>
<LI>Pears</LI>
</OL>
```

Tables

Tables make it possible to set information out in your page as a grid. This can be very useful for presenting number information. Tables can also be used to give more control over the layout of a Web page.

Tables are made up from rows, columns and cells.

To insert a table in FrontPage Express, choose 'Insert Table' from the 'Table' menu.

To change a table choose 'Table Properties' or 'Cell Properties' from the 'Table' menu.

Rows and columns can be added or deleted from a table after it has been created by making selections from the 'Table' menu.

The thickness of the border, padding and spacing of a table can be changed.

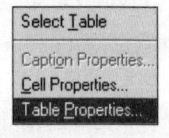

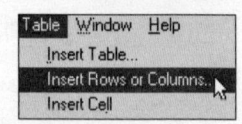

more about HTML

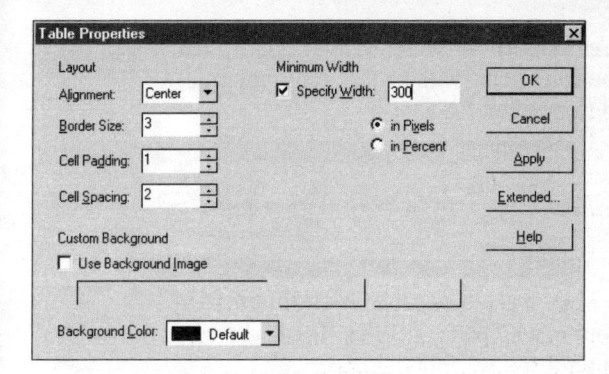

Table Properties dialog:
- Layout
  - Alignment: Center
  - Border Size: 3
  - Cell Padding: 1
  - Cell Spacing: 2
- Minimum Width
  - ☑ Specify Width: 300
  - ○ in Pixels
  - ○ in Percent
- Custom Background
  - ☐ Use Background Image
  - Background Color: Default
- Buttons: OK, Cancel, Apply, Extended..., Help

Padding is the space between the table border and where the content of the table begins.

Spacing is the distance between the separate cells of the table.

The border is a line around the edge of the table.

Tables and the cells inside them can be a fixed size, or can change in relation to the size of the browser window.

Cells can be merged so that they span more than one column or row of cells.

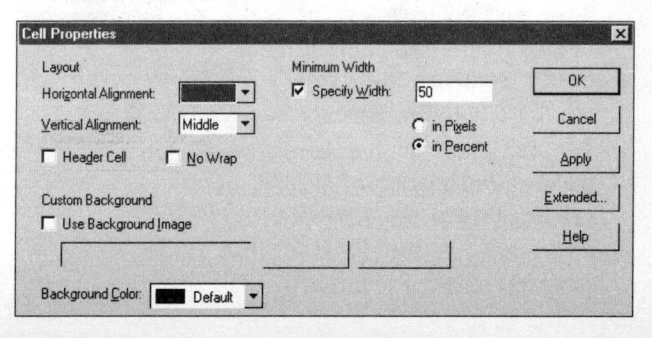

Cell Properties dialog:
- Layout
  - Horizontal Alignment:
  - Vertical Alignment: Middle
  - ☐ Header Cell ☐ No Wrap
- Minimum Width
  - ☑ Specify Width: 50
  - ○ in Pixels
  - ● in Percent
- Custom Background
  - ☐ Use Background Image
  - Background Color: Default
- Buttons: OK, Cancel, Apply, Extended..., Help

Cell heights can be set using the 'extended' button from within the cell properties dialogue box.

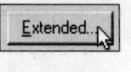

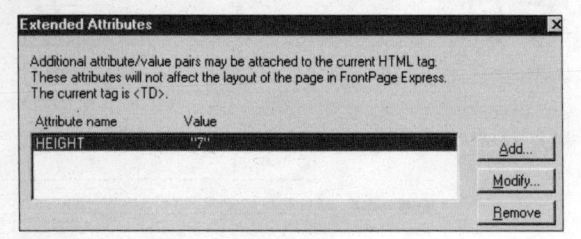

Extended Attributes

Additional attribute/value pairs may be attached to the current HTML tag. These attributes will not affect the layout of the page in FrontPage Express. The current tag is <TD>.

Attribute name	Value
HEIGHT	"7"

Add...
Modify...
Remove

The content of cells can be aligned vertically and horizontally.

There are two tables that you should try to make.

The first is a table to control the position of images on the page. The cells of this table should not have any sizes set for them. They will shrink to the size of the images they contain. The border, padding, and spacing should all be set to 0.

a table created to control the position of images

The second is a table to put text into a grid. Set the width of the table to a percentage of the Window that contains it. Set cell widths to a percentage of the width of the table. The border, padding, and spacing should be set to 1 or more.

a table created for text

Name	Angelo Russell
Age	11
Favourite TV programme	The Net
Favourite sport	Football
Favourite sports personality	Ian Wright
Favourite film star	Whoopi Goldberg
Favourite musicians	Hanson

Frames

Frames are sometimes confused with tables.

Frames are used to sub-divide the browser window so that more than one web page can be displayed at the same time.

Frames are often used to keep a table of contents permanently on view in one frame, while different pages are seen in another frame.

Frames can't be made in FrontPage Express.

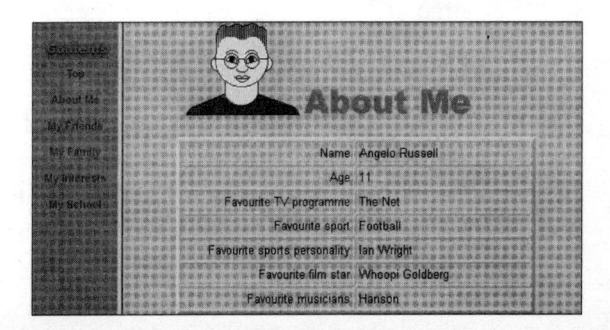

```
<HTML>
 <HEAD>
  <TITLE>Angelo Frameset</TITLE>
 </HEAD>
 <FRAMESET COLS="100,*">
  <FRAME SRC="contents2.htm" NAME="angelo_content"
     SCROLLING=NO NORESIZE>
  <FRAME SRC="angelo2.htm" NAME="angelo_main">
 </FRAMESET>
</HTML>
```

Start by creating a new web page in NotePad. Instead of the <BODY> and </BODY> tags, create <FRAMESET> and </FRAMESET> tags. A page with the <FRAMESET> tag does not contain any information, it only sets which other pages will be loaded into which frame.

You can set the number of columns and the width of each frame using the 'COLS' attribute. You can set fixed column widths in pixels by just entering numbers. Use the % symbol for columns that are relative to the browser window. The * symbol is used to set a column width to fill any remaining space.

To stop frames being moved by the viewer, use the NORESIZE attribute.

The <FRAME> tag is used to set the web pages that will be contained within each frame.

One <FRAME> tag is needed for each column or number in the COLS attribute.

When you click a link in a web page in one frame, you need to be able to set which frame the page being linked to, will load into. This is a two-stage process.

more about HTML

First, each frame needs to be given a name using the NAME attribute in the <FRAME> tag.

Next you will now need to make a new file that will contain links to each page of your web site. See illustration below. This page will appear on the left side of the frameset and will be called 'contents2.htm'. On the page, the <A HREF> links need to be given a *target* attribute to set which frame the new page will be loaded into.

The example shown here is for a common frameset arrangement with a contents page on the left hand side. Try copying it but use your own headings and links.

You have now seen most of the standard ways of creating web pages. Next we will look at adding multimedia files to your web site.

```
<HTML>
<HEAD>
    <TITLE>Contents</TITLE>
</HEAD>
<BODY BGCOLOR="#FF00FF">

<CENTER><B>         </B></CENTER>

<CENTER><BR>
<B><A HREF="angelo2.htm" TARGET="right">Top</A></B></CENTER>

<CENTER><BR>
<B><A HREF="me.htm" TARGET="right">About Me</A></B></CENTER>

<CENTER><BR>
<B><A HREF="myfriends.htm" TARGET="right">My Friends</A></B></CENTER>

<CENTER><BR>
<B><A HREF="myfamily.htm" TARGET="right">My Family</A></B></CENTER>

<CENTER><BR>
<B><A HREF="myinterests.htm" TARGET="right">My Interests</A></B></CENTER>

<CENTER><BR>
<B><A HREF="myschool.htm" TARGET="right">My School</A></B></CENTER>

</BODY>
</HTML>
```

chapter 8
Using sound

This chapter explains how to include sounds on your pages. To understand sound files, a browser needs a separate piece of software called a plug-in. A plug-in for sound is included with recent versions of Navigator and Explorer.

| Top | Me | My Friends | My Family | My Interests | My School |

An audio welcome message

The examples in this section are for GoldWave 4. On the Macintosh you will need SoundEffects 0.9.2 or SoundEdit 16 v2.

Open the software   Goldwave.exe

Create a new file

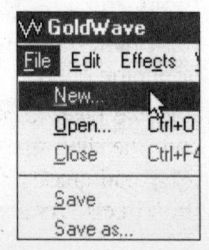

W GoldWave
File Edit Effects
 New...
 Open...   Ctrl+O
 Close   Ctrl+F4
 Save
 Save as...

using sound

Set the software to record at 16 bit mono and a sampling rate of 22050. In GoldWave you need to set a length of time for the sound. In this example it is 5 seconds.

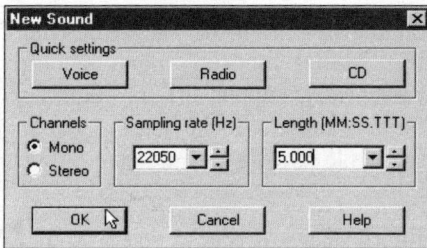

Select 'Device controls' from the 'Tools' menu. A window with recording controls appears. Check that sound is coming into the computer from the microphone. Record a greeting message on your microphone. An image of the soundwave will appear.

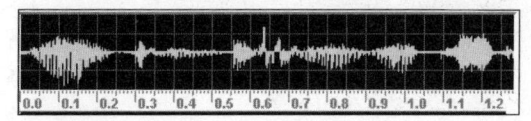

Clip the sound to the exact length that you want without any silent space at the beginning or end.

Now we need to reduce the sound quality and the file size so that the file will download quickly. Choose 'Resample' from the 'Effects' menu.

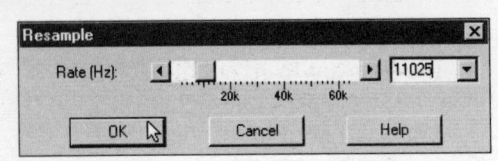

Set the rate to 11025.

Choose save from the file menu. From the format pop-up menu choose Wave(.wav), Apple(.aif) or Sun(.au) format. These are the most common sound file formats for the web.

```
Wave (*.wav)
Voc (*.voc)
Sun (*.au)
Raw (*.snd;*.raw)
Matlab (*.mat)
Apple (*.aif)
Apple-C (*.afc)
Amiga (*.iff)
Dialogic (*.vox)
DiamondWare (*.dwd)
```

The HTML below is what you need to include to set a sound control panel into a web page layout. Put it anywhere between the <BODY> and </BODY> tags.

<EMBED SRC="welcome.au" width="144" height="60" autostart="true" loop="false" hidden="false">

The width and height attributes have been set exactly to the size of the Navigator sound plug-in control panel. 'Autostart' means the sound starts automatically when the page arrives in the browser. In this example the sound is not looping and the control panel is not hidden.

The EMBED tag is not only used for sound files. It is used whenever you want to include a multimedia file format on your web pages.

So now you should have sounds blaring out of your pages. Next we're going to look at how to create some advanced interactivity on your web site.

chapter 9

Adding interactivity

In this chapter you will learn about image-maps, *Common Gateway Interface* (CGI) and *'rollover'* effects.

Image-maps

Image-maps allow you to make different regions of an image link to different pages. We have already made an HTML contents page. Here we will create an alternative contents page with an image-map instead.

First make an image like the one shown here. Call it "contents.gif". Then you will need to look at the HTML below. You should see that there are three parts to an image-map.

```
<HTML>
<HEAD>
 <BASE TARGET="angelo_main">
  <TITLE>Contents</TITLE>
</HEAD>

<BODY BGCOLOR="#ff00ff" BACKGROUND="background3.jpg">

<P ALIGN=CENTER><MAP NAME="          ">

    <AREA SHAPE="rect"  OORDS="1,31,80,52" HREF="angelo2.htm"
TARGET="angelo_main">

    <AREA SHAPE="rect" COORDS="1,56,80,80" HREF="me.htm"
TARGET="angelo_main">

    <AREA SHAPE="rect" COORDS="1,83,80,111"
HREF="myfriends.htm" TARGET="angelo_main">

    <AREA SHAPE="rect" COORDS="1,113,80,137"
HREF="myfamily.htm" TARGET="angelo_main">

    <AREA SHAPE="rect" COORDS="1,141,80,163"
HREF="myinterests.htm" TARGET="angelo_main">

    <AREA SHAPE="rect" COORDS="1,166,80,191"
HREF="myschool.htm" TARGET="angelo_main">

</MAP><IMG SRC="contents.gif" BORDER="0" WIDTH="81"
HEIGHT="191" ALIGN=
"BOTTOM" USEMAP="#contents" ISMAP NATURALSIZEFLAG="0">
</BODY>
</HTML>
```

The first is the <MAP> tag, the second is the <AREA> tag and the last one is the <IMG> tag.

The <MAP> tag contains a set of area tags. It also has a name. <MAP NAME="contents">. Notice that </MAP> appears after the last AREA tag.

The <AREA> tags set all the regions of the image that will be sensitive to a mouse click and where they will link to. In the example here there are six regions. The first one is:

<AREA SHAPE="rect" COORDS="1,31,80,52 HREF="myfriends.htm" TARGET="angelo_main">.

The SHAPE attribute is set to rect - a rectangle. COORDS sets the top left of the rectangle (1 pixel from the left of the image and 31 pixels down) and the bottom right (80 pixels from the left and 52 pixels down). HREF sets which file will be linked to and TARGET is the window frame where the linked file will open.

The <IMG> tag is the usual method for including an image in a page. The difference here is that there are two additional attributes USEMAP and ISMAP. USEMAP="#contents" refers to the name of the map that should be used with this image. This was the name that is given in the <MAP> tag.

There are programmes that you can use to automatically generate co-ordinates for image-maps. See chapter 3 for details.

adding interactivity

CGI

CGI is a scripting language that allows a viewer to send information to your web server. To use CGI we need to make use of *forms*. Angelo's pages include a form for a questionnaire on the environment. Forms can be made up in FrontPage Express using the toolbar. Making forms involves selecting the kind of form element that is required and then inserting ordinary text as questions.

Click the 'One line' field tool to create a box for someone to type their name into. Set the width of the box.

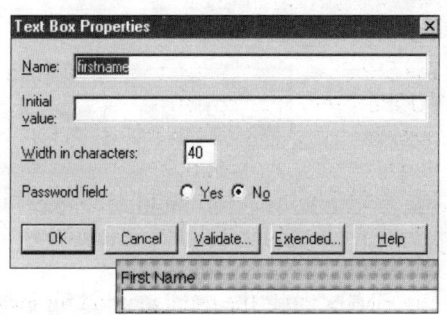

Click the 'pop-up' menu tool and enter the words that you want to appear in the menu.

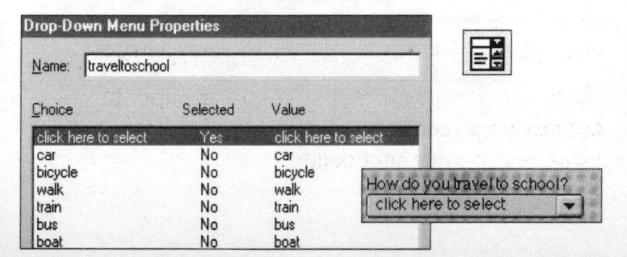

Click the radio button tool and name the button. Naming the button is very important. Radio buttons are used for multiple choice questions where only one answer is allowed. Make sure that all the buttons for one question have the same name. Then set the answer that each button represents in the value field.

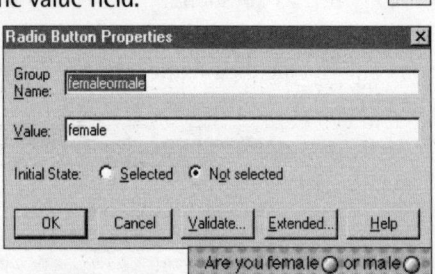

Radio Button Properties

Group Name: femaleormale

Value: female

Initial State: ○ Selected ● Not selected

OK   Cancel   Validate...   Extended...   Help

Are you female ○ or male ○

Use a check box for multiple choice questions where more than one answer is possible.

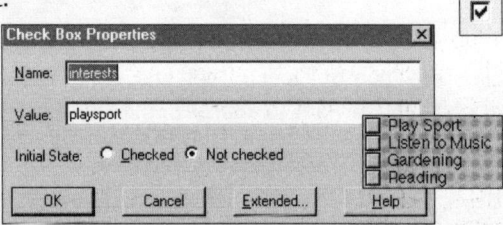

Check Box Properties

Name: interests

Value: playsport

Initial State: ○ Checked ● Not checked

OK   Cancel   Extended...   Help

☐ Play Sport
☐ Listen to Music
☐ Gardening
☐ Reading

adding interactivity

Scrolling fields are used when you don't want written answers of a fixed length.

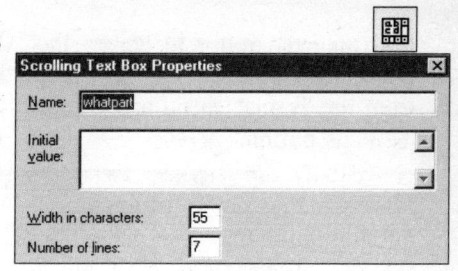

Scrolling Text Box Properties
- Name: whatpart
- Initial value:
- Width in characters: 55
- Number of lines: 7

The submit button is used to send a form to the web server. The reset button allows the user to delete what they have entered onto the form.

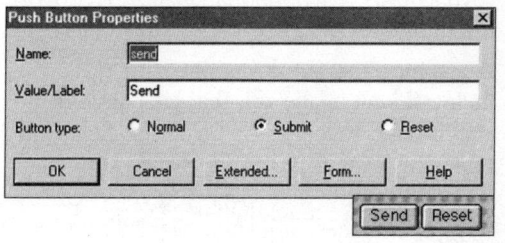

Push Button Properties
- Name: send
- Value/Label: Send
- Button type: ○ Normal ● Submit ○ Reset
- OK | Cancel | Extended... | Form... | Help

[Send] [Reset]

Your *Internet Service Provider* (ISP) will be able to tell you what to include on your web page so that what the viewer enters onto the form can be sent to you. Normally you will need to write something like the following HTML: <FORM ACTION="cgi-bin/mailform" METHOD="GET">

In this example the CGI script that processes the form is called 'mailform' and is in a directory called 'cgi-bin'.

In 'Explorer' you can enter this CGI information by selecting 'Form properties' from the 'Format' menu and choosing the 'Settings' button.

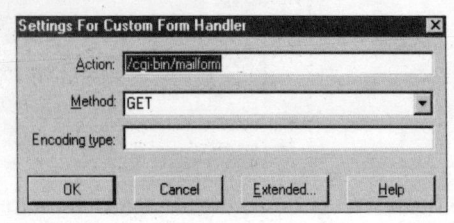

JavaScript

JavaScript is a *scripting* language that was introduced by Netscape.

A common use for Javascript is to make a 'rollover' - an image link that changes when the mouse touches it. 'Rollovers' help to highlight areas that can be clicked with the mouse. To create a 'rollover' you will need to have two images with some slight difference between them. In this example the first is a still image and the second an animated one. When the pointer moves over the first image the second one replaces it so that it appears to start moving. When the pointer moves off the image the original image loads back in again.

adding interactivity

The first thing you need to do for a 'rollover' is to put a script like this one between the <HEAD> and </HEAD> tags.

```
<SCRIPT LANGUAGE="JavaScript">
if (document.images) {
 var firston = new Image();
 firston.src = "fullangeloanim.gif";
 var secondon = new Image();
 secondon.src = "spinninga.gif";
 }

function secondimage() {
if (document.images)
document.images.spinninga.src = secondon.src;
 }

function firstimage() {
if (document.images)
document.images.spinninga.src = firston.src;
 }
//
</SCRIPT>
```

The second part goes into an <A> tag and an <IMG> tag.

```
<A  HREF="angframe2.htm" onMouseOver="secondimage()"
onMouseOut="firstimage()">
<IMG SRC="fullangeloanim.gif" NAME="spinninga" BORDER="0"
ALT="Image of Angelo"></A>
```

For a 'rollover' an image is used as a link. The <IMG> tag appears where the text would usually be. When you create a 'rollover', you will need to use your own images instead of 'fullangeloanim.gif' and 'spinninga.gif'.

You will also want to replace the word 'spinninga' wherever it appears. Instead of: NAME="spinninga" and 'document.images.spinninga.src', you might have:

NAME="myrollover" and
'document.images.myrollover.src'.

Javascript and CGI are some of the most advanced parts of creating web pages. From now on it's plain sailing all the way until your pages are on-line.

chapter 10
Uploading your web site

Here are the last few things you will need to do to finally get your pages on-line.

Publicising your web site

You can tell your friends about your web site, but if you want to get the attention of a wider audience, you need to get it listed on-line. *Search Engines* are computers that index world wide web pages. You can wait for a search engine to find your pages, but to speed the process up, try submitting your pages at the following addresses:

www.lycos.com/search/addasite.html

www.hotbot.com/addurl.html

www.excite.com/Info/add_url.html

www.infoseek.com

There are many different search engines and it can take time to contact them all, so some companies do all the work for you. Limited, free services are available at:

www.register-it.com

free.submit-it.com

Search engines index words that you write in the <TITLE> tag of your pages. So think carefully about the titles you choose. You can also hint about other key words that you think are important by using the <META> tag. Create something like the following tag in the <HEAD> section of your pages:

```
<META NAME="description" CONTENT="The famous
web pages of Angelo Russell">.
<META NAME="keywords" CONTENT="angelo, russell,
children, child, survey, family, friends, art, gallery,
stories">
```

Getting hold of web space

To be on the Internet, web pages need to be stored on computers called web servers. You can rent web space or you might be able to use it free of charge.

Do you know someone, perhaps your parent, a friend or a relation who can let you use web space where they work? Another possibility would be to ask your school if they have access to a web server. Alternatively you can usually get access to web space at no extra cost through the company that connects your home to the Internet. Leading ISPs in the UK include:

Demon Internet Telephone 0181 371 1000

EasyNet Telephone 0541 594 321

Global Internet Telephone 0870 909 8000

Pipex Dial Telephone 0500 474 739

Before you upload your pages there are some important things that you should check.

Naming files

Check that all your file names are in lower case and that you have not used any spaces. Also make sure that every file has the correct suffix (.htm, .gif, .jpg).

You should also consider using a default file name for your first page or home page. This makes it easier for people to remember your web site address. Instead of having to remember:

'www.demon.co.uk/angelowebsite/angelo.htm'

they only need to remember:

'www.demon.co.uk/angelowebsite'

and the default file will then load in automatically. Check with your ISP to find out how to name the default file. Examples are index.htm, index.html. If you change the name of your first page to one of these, make sure that you update any pages that link back to it.

Image file size

Make sure that every image has a file size that is as small as it can be without losing too much quality. See methods for reducing image file sizes in chapter 6. The directory that contains your web site may include files that are no longer needed. These should not be put on the web server.

Check the size of your web site

Click onto the folder that contains your final project. If you are using a Macintosh choose 'Get Info' from the 'File' menu. If you are using Windows 95/98 choose 'Properties' from the

'File' menu. If you are using Windows 3.1 look at the bottom of the file manager window. Check how many bytes are being used for the folder. Divide the total in the folder by the number of pages in your web site. This tells you how big an average page is. Ideally you should not use more than 30k per page.

Checking links and images

Before you get your pages on-line you need to test them. Create a new directory or folder on your computer and copy your files into it. Then open your home page into your web browser and check the links and images on every page. If you find any errors, note them down and then carry on with the rest of the checking.

When you have reached the end, open your HTML editor and correct the errors. Then go back and check the pages again.

Missing images

You can work out why an image hasn't loaded by looking at the icon that appears in its place.

One indicates that an image has been found but cannot be read, the other that an image cannot be found at all.

If the image has been found but cannot be read, this is a problem with the file format. Perhaps you have given the file the suffix '.gif' when it is really a JPEG file or vice versa.

Broken links

There are three reasons why a link might not work:

- The file name in the HTML link may not match the actual document name that it refers to
- The file may be missing altogether
- The file might not be a correct HTML file.

Checking pages on different operating systems and web browsers

Different web browsers support slightly different versions of HTML. You should ideally check how your pages look on a range of different browsers and computers.

Contacting you

It is a good idea to include the following HTML at the bottom of your pages. If anyone finds errors on your pages, they can let you know about them by e-mail:

<AHREF="mailto:angelo@demon.co.uk">
Click here if you want to report any errors on my pages </A>.

Uploading your pages

Once your pages are tested you can copy them onto a web server.

uploading your web site

If you are working at school or in an office, you may be able to copy your files to the web server over a local computer network. If you access the Internet through a dial-up account, you will need a File Transfer Protocol (FTP) programme. You can use Fetch if you are working on a Macintosh, or CuteFTP if you have a PC.

Open your FTP software.

From the 'FTP' menu, choose 'Quick Connect'.

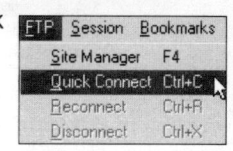

Enter the log-in details of the server that you are trying to connect to. If you don't know them, check with your ISP.

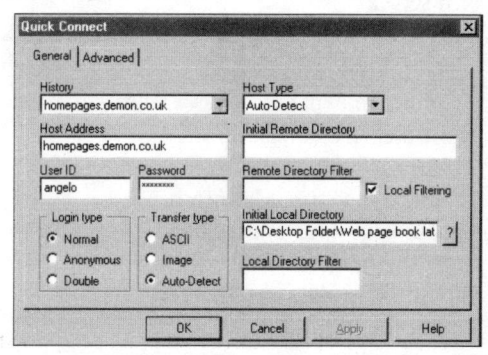

You can also choose where files are going to come from on your computer.

STATUS:> Connecting homepages.demon.co.uk

You may see some commands flashing up as the software logs into the web server. Then a window will appear that shows your directory.

C: ▾	c:\desktop folder\ ▾	/u/demon.co.uk/ ▾
📁 angelowebsite		📁 ..

In CuteFTP you can drag files from the left panel to the right panel to move them from your hard disk to the web server.

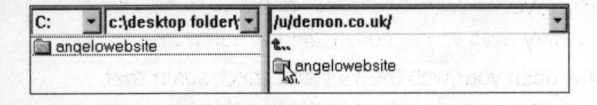

C: ▾	c:\desktop folder\ ▾	/u/demon.co.uk/ ▾
📁 angelowebsite		📁 ..
		📁 angelowebsite

In Fetch on the Macintosh, Choose 'put files and folders' from the 'remote' menu. Then choose 'Raw data' as the file format for each file.

uploading your web site

Once the files appear on the web server you should check that the access privileges or file attributes are set as shown. Choose them from the 'Command' menu.

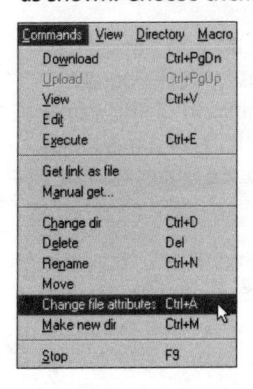

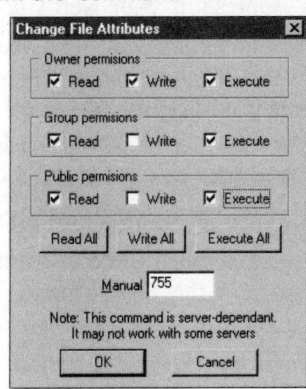

Some ISPs set them for you automatically, so you may not be able to change them.

Before you view your pages on the web browser you may need to log out of the FTP software.

Now open your web browser and check again that all of your pages work correctly but this time you will need to access them from the web server, not from your computer's hard disk. Your ISP will tell you the address for your pages.

Hooray! You've now published your pages on the Internet.

Hopefully this is just the first in a long line of great web sites. The next chapter gives you some ideas about how you might want to develop your web authoring skills.

chapter 11
Where to go from here

Here are some more topics that you might wish to explore.

Improving your web site

One important way that a web site differs from a book is that it can be changed more easily. Once your web site is on-line, that's only the beginning of the story. Now you need to keep it up-to-date. Your aim should be to keep visitors coming back to see what's new.

Learning more about HTML

There is much more to learn about HTML than the space in this book allowed. There is also an endless amount to learn about working with multimedia file formats to make your pages more interesting, entertaining and exciting.

Using HTML 4

This book has concentrated on HTML 3. You may want to go on to learn about some of the changes in HTML 4 next. Look at the HTML 4 specifications at www.w3.org

Hosting your own web site

One way to develop your Internet skills is to learn how to manage a web server yourself. To do this you need access to a permanent connection to the Internet.

Competition

For details of our competition for the best web site created by someone who has used this book, go to www.bloomsbury.com/websitebook

Good luck with all your future web authoring exploits.

glossary

Absolute link - A link to a particular place on the Internet using the full URL.

Anchor - Text or images that can be clicked on, to link to another page.

Anti-alias - A process that smoothes the edges of text.

Attributes - Part of HTML that sets how a tag will work.

Background - The area of a web page behind the text.

Banner - A shape for an image that can be used as a heading or advert on a web page.

Bookmark - The term used in FrontPage Express for a marker on a page that can be linked to.

Browser - A programme used to look at web pages.

Cell - An individual section of a table on a web page.

CGI - See Common Gateway Interface.

Column - Part of an HTML table.

Common Gateway Interface - Scripting system that can provide visitors to web pages with customised information.

Compression - The process of squeezing data into a smaller space.

Flat Colour - Colour with only one shade.

Forms - A part of HTML that allows the viewer to send information back to the web server.

Frames - A method for showing several web pages in one window.

GIF - A file format used for flat colour graphics.

Hexadecimal - The numbering system used to set the colours that will be used in a web page.

Hierarchic - A structure for a web site that gives the viewer choices.

Home Page - The first page reached by a visitor to a web site.

House Style - A set of rules for the design of your web site.

HTML - Hyper Text Markup Language. The language of web pages.

Hyper Text Markup Language - HTML - the language used to create web pages.

Hypertext - Text that can be clicked to move to another page.

Image-Map - An image with zones that link to different pages depending on where you click.

Indent - Where the text on a web page is moved to the right.

Indexed colour - A way of storing the colour information in an image so that it takes up less space.

Interactivity - Where the viewer of a web page is able to control and get feedback about what they are doing.

Internet - The international system for exchanging information over computer networks.

Internet Service Provider - A company that connects you to the Internet and provides web space.

ISP - See Internet Service Provider.

Javascript - A scripting language that can be used to create interactive effects on web pages.

JPEG - A file format used for photographic images.

Linear - A web site structure where there are no choices about which route to take.

glossary

Link - A connection to another page.

Lower case - Writing without using capital letters is recommended for web page file names.

Modem - A device for connecting to the Internet using a telephone line.

Multimedia - Sound, text, video and still images presented on a computer.

Pixel - A tiny square that makes up a computer image.

Plug-In - Software that allows a browser to read multimedia files.

Protocol - An system for exchanging information on the Internet. The protocol for the Web is 'http'.

Relative link - A link to a local file.

Rollover - An animation effect that happens when the mouse moves onto a link.

Row - Part of an HTML table.

Rules - A horizontal line that can be placed into a web page layout.

Scripting - Programming that makes web pages more interactive. Examples include CGI and Javascript.

Search Engine - A computer that indexes the Web.

Suffix - An addition to the end of a file name. Examples include '.gif', '.jpg', '.htm'.

Table - A way of organising information into rows and columns.

Tag - A piece of HTML code.

Target - The term used in Netscape Composer for a marker on a page that can be linked to.

The Web - Short for World Wide Web.

Tonal image - An image that has many different shades or colours.
Uniform Resource Locator - The method used to describe the location of a file on the Internet.
Upper case - Text written in capital letters.
URL - See Uniform Resource Locator.
Visitors - A term used in this book to describe anyone looking at a web page.
Web Page - A single document on the World Wide Web.
Web Safe Colour - A set of 216 hexadecimal colours that display accurately on monitors set to 256 colours.
Web Server - A computer that stores web pages.
Web Site - A collection of web pages.
Web Space - Storage for web pages.
Web - Short for the World Wide Web.
WWW - Short for World Wide Web.
World Wide Web - A system of interconnected pages on the Internet.
WYSIWYG - 'What you see is what you get'.